It's Easy To Play Pop Hits.

Wise Publications
London / New York / Paris / Sydney / Copenhagen / Madrid / Tokyo

Exclusive Distributors:

Music Sales Limited
8/9 Frith Street, London W1V 5TZ, England.

Music Sales Pty Limited
120 Rothschild Avenue, Rosebery, NSW 2018, Australia.

Order No. AM956219
ISBN 0-7119-8206-6
This book © Copyright 2000 by Wise Publications.

Cover photographs courtesy of All Action & London Features International.
Compiled by Nick Crispin.
Music arranged by Stephen Duro.
Music processed by Allegro Reproductions.

Music Sales' complete catalogue describes thousands of titles and
is available in full colour sections by subject, direct from Music Sales Limited.
Please state your areas of interest and send a cheque/postal order for £1.50 for postage to:
Music Sales Limited, Newmarket Road, Bury St. Edmunds, Suffolk IP33 3YB.

www.musicsales.com

Your Guarantee of Quality:
As publishers, we strive to produce every book to the highest commercial standards.
The music has been freshly engraved and the book has been carefully designed to minimise awkward page turns and to make playing from it a real pleasure.
Particular care has been given to specifying acid-free, neutral-sized paper made from pulps which have not been elemental chlorine bleached.
This pulp is from farmed sustainable forests and was produced with special regard for the environment.
Throughout, the printing and binding have been planned to ensure a sturdy, attractive publication which should give years of enjoyment.
If your copy fails to meet our high standards, please inform us and we will gladly replace it.

Printed in the United Kingdom by
Caligraving Limited, Thetford, Norfolk.

American Pie

Words & Music by Don McLean

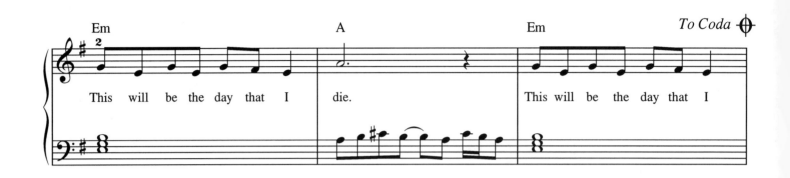

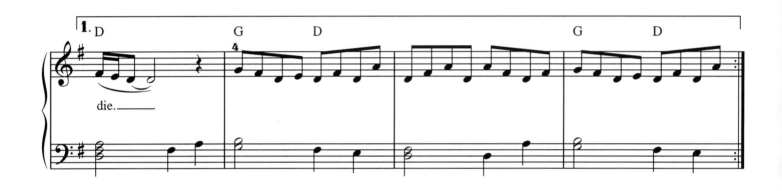

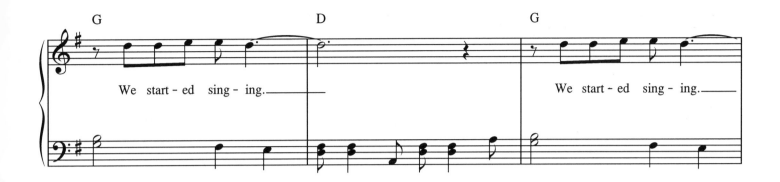

We start - ed sing - ing._____ We start - ed sing - ing._____

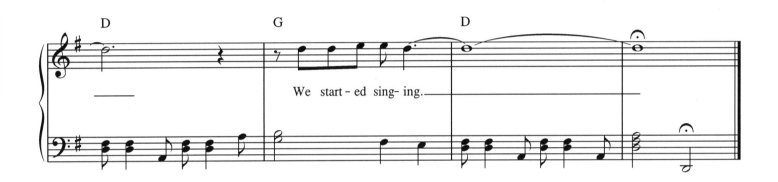

_____ We start - ed sing- ing._____

Verse 2:

I met a girl who sang the blues
And I asked her for some happy news
But she just smiled and turned away
Well I went down to the sacred store
Where I'd heard the music years before
But the man there said the music wouldn't play
Well now in the streets the children screamed
The lovers cried and the poets dreamed
But not a word was spoken
The church bells all were broken
And the three men I admire the most
The Father, Son and the Holy Ghost
They caught the last train for the coast
The day the music died
We started singing.

Bye-bye Miss American Pie *etc.*

Fool Again

Words & Music by Jörgen Elofsson, Per Magnusson & David Kreuger

Moderately

1. Ba - by, I know the sto - ry, I've seen the
mf *(Verse 2 see block lyric)*
pic - ture, it's writ - ten all ov - er your face. Tell me, what's the
se - cret that you've been hid - ing, and who's gon - na take my place? I
should - 've seen it com - ing, I should - 've read the signs. A - ny-

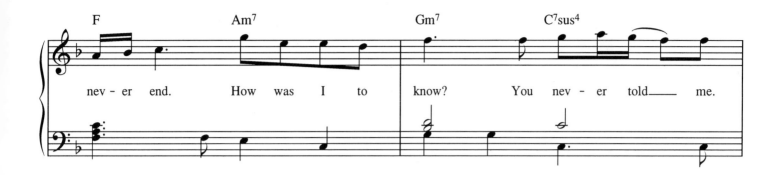

nev - er end. How was I to know? You nev - er told___ me.

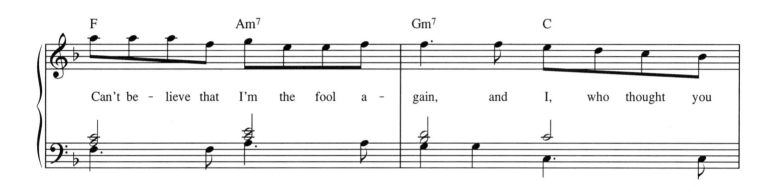

Can't be - lieve that I'm the fool a - gain, and I, who thought you

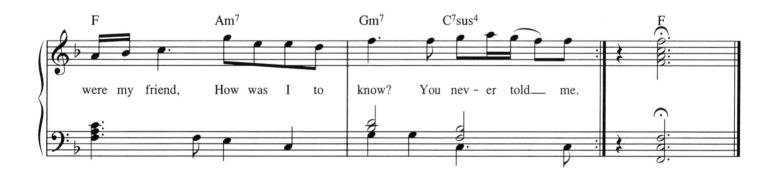

were my friend, How was I to know? You nev - er told___ me.

Verse 2:

Baby, you should've called me
When you were lonely
When you needed me to be there
Sadly, you never gave me
Too many chances
To show you how much I care.

I should've seen it coming *etc.*

Born To Make You Happy

Words & Music by Andreas Carlsson & Kristian Lundin

Moderately

mf 1. I'm sit - ting here a - lone up in my room,
(Verse 2 see block lyric)

and think - in' 'bout the times that we've been through, oh, my love.

I'm look - ing at a pic - ture in my hand, try - ing my best to un - der -

- stand. I real - ly want to know what we did wrong with a love that felt so

Just to   show you how much___ I___ care.

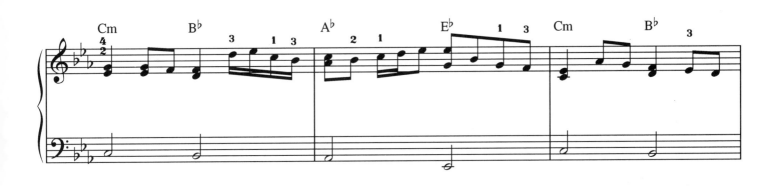

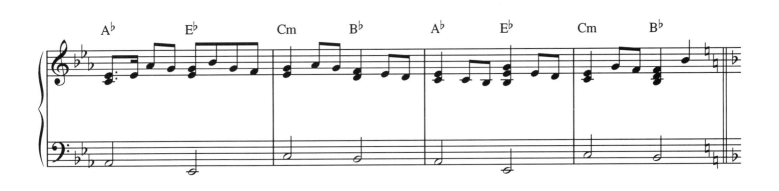

I   don't know how to live with - out your   love, I was born to make you hap - py.

'Cause you're the on-ly one with-in my heart, I was born to make you hap-py.

Al-ways and for-ev-er you and me, that's the way our life should

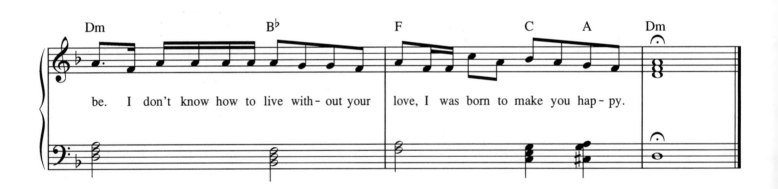

be. I don't know how to live with-out your love, I was born to make you hap-py.

Verse 2:

I know I've been a fool since you've been gone
I'd better give it up and carry on, oh my love
'Cause living in a dream of you and me is not the way my life should be
I don't want to cry a tear for you so forgive me if I do.

If only you were here tonight *etc.*

If I Could Turn Back The Hands Of Time

Words & Music by R. Kelly

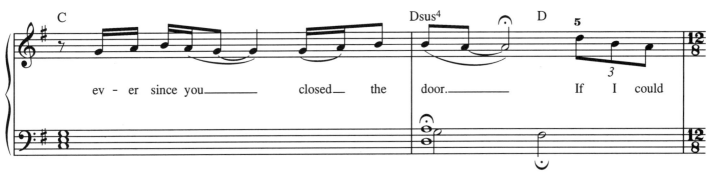

19

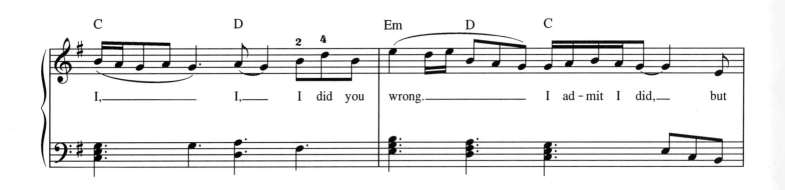

I,_____ I,_____ I did you wrong._____ I ad - mit I did,_____ but

now_____ I'm fac - ing the rest of my life a - lone.____

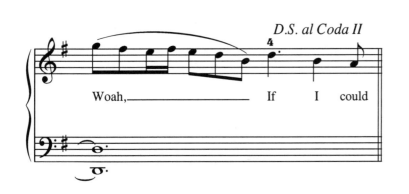

D.S. al Coda II

Woah,_____ If I could

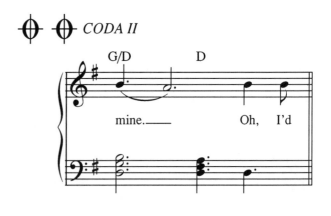

CODA II

mine.____ Oh, I'd

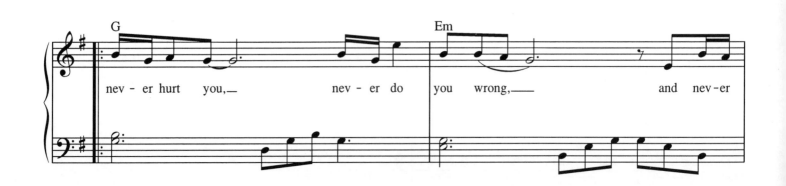

nev - er hurt you,_____ nev - er do you wrong,_____ and nev - er

leave your side.___ Turn back the hands.___ Woah,_____ I'd

hands.___ Love you. (If I could turn back.)

Repeat to fade

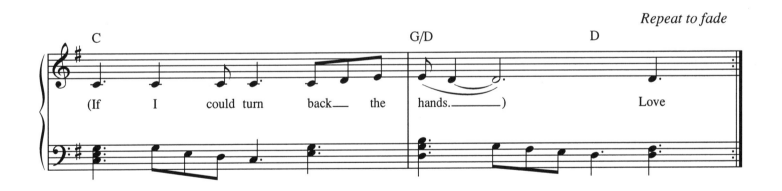

(If I could turn back___ the hands._____) Love

3°:

Woah, if I could just turn back that little clock on the wall
Then I'd come to realise how much I love you.

I Try

Words by Macy Gray
Music by Macy Gray, Jeremy Ruzumna, Jinsoo Lim & David Wilder

touch, your love, kiss - es and such. With all my might I try, but this I can't de-

- ny, de - ny.___ I play it off, but I'm dream -

D.S. Repeat to fade

- ing of you.___ And I'll keep my cool but I'm fiend - ing. I try to say good-

Verse 2:

I may appear to be free
But I'm just a prisoner of your love
And I may seem alright
And smile when you leave
But my smiles are just a front, just a front
Hey! I play it off, but I'm dreaming of you
And I'll keep my cool but I'm fiending.

I try to say goodbye and I choke *etc.*

I Wouldn't Believe Your Radio

Words by Kelly Jones
Music by Kelly Jones, Richard Jones & Stuart Cable

27

You can have it all if you like,— and you can pay for it the rest of your—

— li - - i - i - i - ife.—

Li - - i - i - i - ife.—

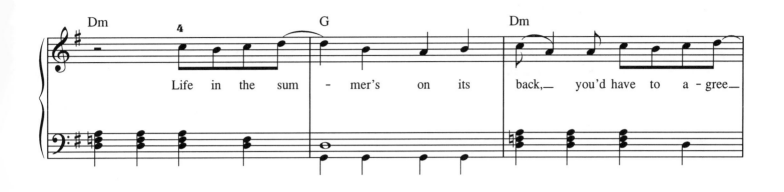

Life in the sum - mer's on its back, you'd have to a - gree

that that's the crack, so take what you want, I'm not com - ing

back. So you can have it

all if you like.

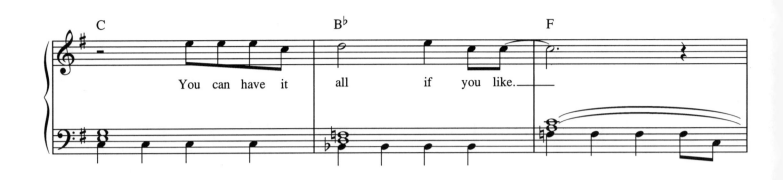

You can have it all if you like.

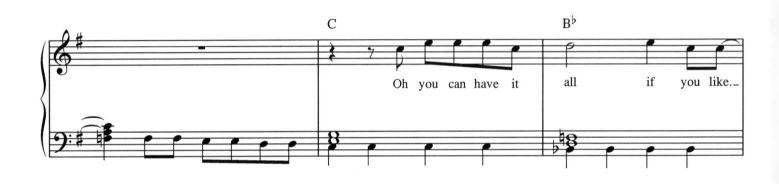

Oh you can have it all if you like.

You can have it

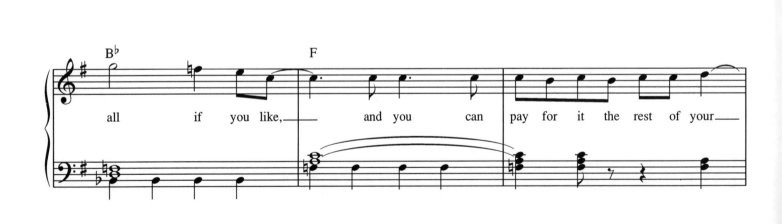

all if you like, and you can pay for it the rest of your

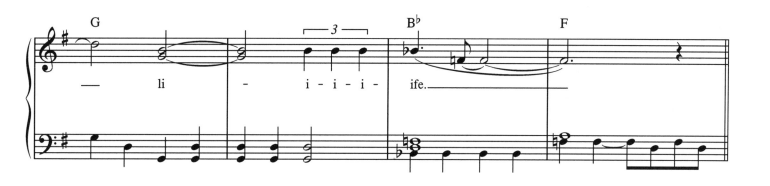

— li - - i - i - i - ife._____

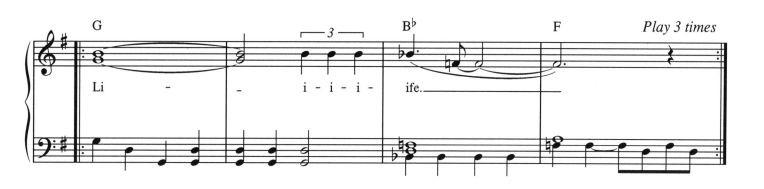

Li - - i - i - i - ife._____

Play 3 times

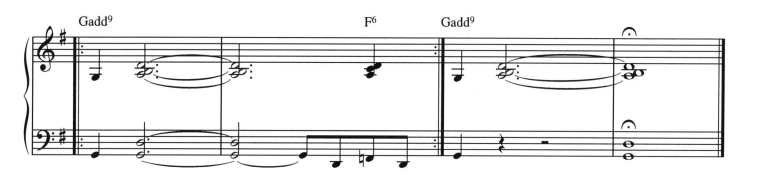

Verse 2:

I wouldn't believe your wireless radio
If I had myself a flying giraffe
You'd have one in a box with a window.

But you can have it all *etc.*

Lift Me Up

Words & Music by Geri Halliwell, Andy Watkins, Paul Wilson & Tracy Ackerman

when the day is ov - er, when the sun
when the lights are fad - ing, when I'm fly -

— is go - ing down, I will be your an - gel now.
- ing way up high, and I'll be

1.

2. Lift me up your an - gel for life.

Your an - gel for life.

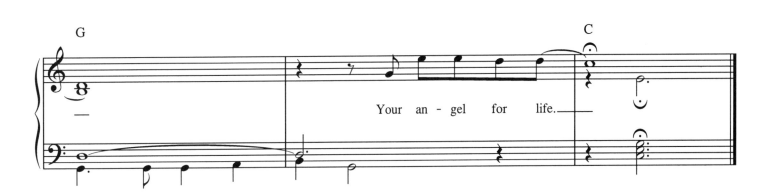

Verse 2:

Like the seasons, ever changing
Everlasting, baby, like you and I
It's gonna be alright
But when my sky clouds over

Lift me up *etc.*

Rise

Words & Music by Bob Dylan, Gabrielle, Ferdy Unger-Hamilton & Ollie Dagois

Moderately

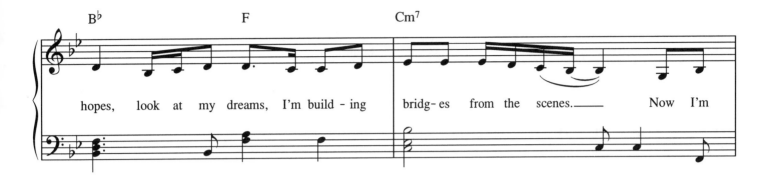

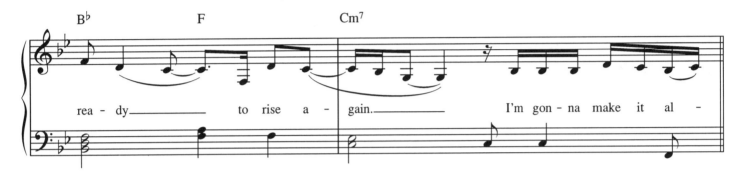

Verse 2:

Caught up in my thinking
Like a prisoner in my mind
You pose so many questions
That the truth is hard to find
I'd better think twice I know
That I'll get over you.

Look at my life *etc.*

Turn

Words & Music by Fran Healy

41

oh_____ hi._____

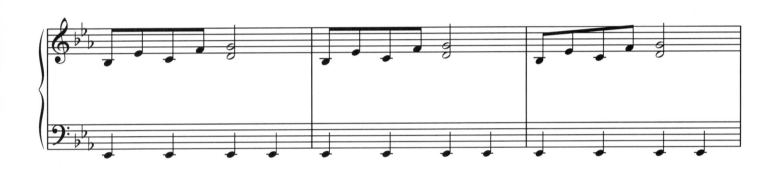

Verse 2:

So where's the stars? Up in the sky
And what's the moon? A big balloon
We'll never know unless we grow
There's so much world outside the door.

I want to sing, to sing my song
I want to live in a world where I'll be strong
I want to live, I will survive
And I believe that it won't be very long.

Never Be The Same Again

Words & Music by Melanie Chisholm, Rhett Lawrence, Paul F. Cruz, Lisa Lopes & Lorenzo Martin

Nite and day | Black beach sand to red clay to the | US to UK, NYC to LA from sidewalks to

highways. See it'll never be the same, what I'm sayin' | my mind frame never changed 'til you came and rearranged but

sometimes it seems completely forbidden to discover | those feelings that we kept so well hidden where there's
A fine line's between fate and destiny. Do you believe | in the things that were just meant to be? When you
energies mix and begin to multiply everyday situations, | they start to simplify so

Play 3 times

no competition and you render my condition though improbable | it's not impossible for a love that could be unstoppable but wait.
tell me the stories of your quest for me, picturesque is the picture | you paint effortlessly and as our
things will never be the same between you and I we intertwined | our life forces and now we're unified.

⊕ *CODA*

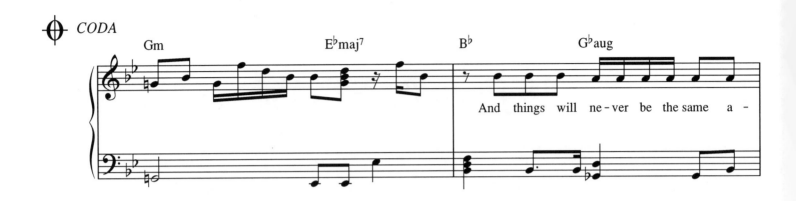

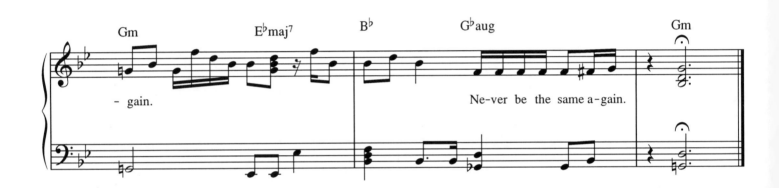

Verse 2:

Now I know that we were close before
I'm glad I realised I need you so much more
And I don't care what everyone will say
It's about you and me
And we'll never be the same again.

I thought that we would just be friends   *etc.*